Clara French

The dramatic action and motive of King John

Clara French

The dramatic action and motive of King John

ISBN/EAN: 9783743377325

Manufactured in Europe, USA, Canada, Australia, Japa

Cover: Foto ©ninafisch / pixelio.de

Manufactured and distributed by brebook publishing software (www.brebook.com)

Clara French

The dramatic action and motive of King John

THE DRAMATIC ACTION AND MOTIVE OF KING JOHN

An Essay

BY

CLARA FRENCH, A. M.

WITH A MEMORIAL SKETCH OF THE WRITER

CAMBRIDGE
Printed at the Riverside Press
1892

Copyright, 1892,
By MARY E. W. FRENCH.

> The sun nor loiters nor speeds,
>   The rivers run as they ran,
> Through clouds or through windy reeds
>   All run as when all began.
> Only Death turns at our cries:—
> Lo, the Hope we buried with sighs
> Alive in Death's eyes!
>
> CHRISTINA ROSSETTI.

CLARA FRENCH

CLARA FRENCH

The life of Clara French held more of promise than of fulfillment. Her nature was strong in patience, her force spent in serious and quiet preparation. Thus, when in the autumn of 1888 she was called to the higher and celestial service, she had but just entered upon that vocation of teacher at Wellesley College to which she looked forward with loyal earnestness as the beginning of her life-work. She left behind her small record of obvious achievement, or of definite lines of outward activity. Her activities were within her own spirit, her achievements rather in character than in deed. Of the inner workings of such a life as hers, little can be said. Its secrets are hidden with the mystery of that great underworld of latent forces which slowly, in darkness and silence, work their way to self-expression. No one more than Clara French would dread any approach to publicity; and none whose lives were near her own could now seek to violate the noble reticence which set her apart from others by a peculiar dignity. Yet, for the sake of the many who honor her, it is fitting that one example of her genuine and scholarly work be preserved; and such an example will tell its story better if prefaced by a few notes concerning her outward life and a few suggestions concerning the growth of the mind and spirit within.

Clara French was born July 30, 1863, in Syracuse, New York. She was the only living daughter of John H. French, LL. D., honorably identified for many years with educational work of various kinds. Before she was four years old, the family removed to Albany, New York. When she was seven they went to Burlington, Vermont, where the rare beauty of lake and mountain sank deep into the child's nature, and gave her a feeling of home to which she returned with clinging affection of memory through all her later years.

A friend writes about her as a little girl: " No child ever played with heartier enjoyment than Clara. One of memory's pleasantest pictures is her glowing face as she came in to tell me of the fine time she had been having with her sled. She did not care so much for the society of children of her own age in the house. She preferred to "help me" about my work as secretary to her father.

"One of her most noticeable traits as a little child was her interest in everything about her. She was never dull. There was a bright, alert expression in her face that kept you constantly expecting something. Her progress was steady. She was able to concentrate her attention upon a subject at will. She wasted no time vacillating, but decided to do a thing and went directly and simply about it. As might be expected, she was remarkably truthful."

Eager interest in living, energy, decision, and sincerity — these, as they marked her character at the beginning, remained with her to the end. Almost the same traits are signaled in a letter from another friend, written about her later girlhood : —

"I was strongly impressed with her truthfulness, honesty, conscientiousness, and purity of thought and act. She was introspective and analytical, even at that age, and studied her motives of thought and deed. I believe her inmost thought could bear the strongest sunlight. Clara was sensitive, and ardent in her affections. Her sympathy with the sad and sorrowing was expressed less by words and tears than by her deep silence. This silence was one of her peculiarities; it was a silence of her whole being, and in it lay much of her power. She was, in general, reticent relative to her own convictions and emotions.

"Clara's lessons were a pastime rather than a task. Her clear, incisive intellect seemed to penetrate at a glance to the very depth of the author's meaning. She knew nothing of intellectual toil or effort in those days.

"Clara's acquaintance with natural sciences — mineralogy in particular — was quite remarkable in one so young. She had a little cabinet which was her special pride. She delighted in giving me her little 'lectures' upon her 'stones.' 'Flowers are sweet and pretty,' she said, 'but not so pretty as stones. I love stones best.' At the age of fourteen, she assisted in classifying and arranging the cabinet in the Mansfield, Pa., Normal School. Her interest in this subject grew steadily. Her collection had become quite large before she entered college, and I could not but feel and express regret when I found her attention diverted to literature. I had looked for her to make rapid strides in the sciences, and I believe the change was not made without many misgivings and regrets on her part."

A significant period in Clara's life was spent at Indiana, Pa., whither the family moved in 1878. Here she prepared for college in the Normal School of which her father was principal. In 1880 she returned to her beloved Burlington, where she took her Freshman year at the University of Vermont. During this year she was confirmed in the Episcopal Church, of which her parents were members. In the autumn of her Sophomore year, she entered Smith College, where she was graduated in June, 1884. A year of graduate study in literature at Oxford, England, was followed by a year and a half of teaching in the Normal School at New Paltz, Ulster County, New York. The winter of 1887-88 she spent at Cornell, where she received the Master's degree in the spring. In September, 1888, she went to Wellesley College, where she had been appointed instructor in the department of English literature. After less than two weeks of work, she was stricken with typhoid fever, and died on the 6th of October. She was twenty-five years old.

No life could have been more outwardly uneventful. Passed almost entirely within college walls, it knew no obvious excitement or romance : passed, with the exception of a year and a half, in distinct preparation, it was to all seeming broken short at the very moment of fulfillment. Yet the quiet years were full of eager outreaching toward the two supreme realities of Truth and Passion ; and to those who knew her best, the life was manifest as a completed whole, in which a noble and definite development was perfectly achieved.

Of Clara French's brief twenty-five years of earthly life, the most critical and decisive were probably those which she spent at Smith College, Northampton, Mass.

Women's opportunities for a broader education were then comparatively new, and women's colleges had not yet passed out of the experimental stage. The conditions of life which they offered were in some ways singularly interesting. Simpler in many respects than at present, and inferior in scholarly equipment to the colleges of to-day, they were yet permeated by a spirit of fresh enthusiasm and high ambition which went far to compensate for defects in machinery. The three hundred students gathered at Northampton were athirst for wisdom and for experience. They were mostly from New England, and the moral strenuousness of the old New England stock showed itself sometimes in an over-minute excitability of conscience. They were modern girls, with the modern impulse to challenge the foundations of faith and to analyze the finest fibres of character. It was natural that a certain tendency to exaltation and morbid introspection should not always be avoided. But any unfortunate elements in the life were largely counteracted by the sane and inspiring beauty of the surrounding nature, by the wise guidance of certain Professors, and by the vistas into world-wisdom as well as into world-problem constantly opened through study. In this vivid young community, Clara French soon became a prominent figure. She was strong, effective, self-possessed, with a large and easy cleverness that commanded notice. Although a mere girl, she already, by appearance and manner, gave the impression of maturity. This impression, however, was misleading. She had awakened before she came to that self-consciousness which is always tumultuous and chaotic with strong natures in youth. In spite of her outward quietude, she had not yet found her true self; and the intensity of her nature threatened in those days to be self-consuming. Uncontrolled except by surface stoicism, conflicting forces drove her through her college years from phase to phase of experience. Her intellectual life was as yet comparatively undeveloped. Books, of course, were devoured: Carlyle, Emerson, Shelley, George Eliot, Arnold, Clough, and — he was a discovery in those days — Browning. Classwork opened the way for endless discussions of the great problems, psychological, theological, social, which are usually attacked with audacity in inverse ratio to age. But it yet remained true, as it had been true in childhood, that intellectual effort was unknown to Clara French. She was content to rest in her instinctive and natural power, and she knew as yet nothing of absorption in the pursuit of abstract truth, or of that disinterested devotion to pure scholarship which was to form so large a factor in her later life. The line of her conscious development in those years was mainly ethical. They were years of growth and struggle. Life was no easy task to her, then or ever, but she met it with high courage. She did not carry away from Smith College a disciplined or perhaps even a thoroughly awakened intellect; but she carried away something better, a character of which the trend towards selfless nobility, towards controlled consecration, was determined once for all. A few words of her own, written just before her Senior year, tell simply and earnestly how inestimable a debt she felt herself to owe to her Alma Mater.

"I'm going to hunt up something vigorous to read. I feel all let down mentally.

"*Later.* Joshua and Paul proved vigorous enough for my wants. I should like to write about Joshua.

"One thing has suggested another, and something has just come back to me which I had hardly thought of since it happened. I can remember perfectly the bright September morning, two years ago, when I took my first look over the college grounds. I was entirely alone, and except for one or two bowing acquaintances I knew no one there. I remember wondering what my life there would be, and thinking all the vague thoughts that come into one's mind at such a time. How far away it all seems now! If there is one thing above everything else in my life for which I am, I trust, truly and humbly grateful, it is that that September morning found me where it did. That all our plans were guided as they were gives me new hope and strength. For whatever sadness has come to me I can only be thankful, for with it has come a sweetness and a seriousness that probably could not have come in any other way."

A few extracts from her letters, written in the summer after her Senior year, will give suggestions of her outlook, interests, and ambitions, at the trying time when the conventional training is over, and the young life has to decide for itself "What next?" It will be seen that Clara French was not lacking in cheery courage, sound common-sense, and firmly-held purpose: —

"You would have liked the clouds that I watched this morning, as I was dressing for church. They were dazzlingly white, the nearest ones, and they moved very fast; and they curled a little piece of themselves back, every little way, to show the delicate clouds that had tried to keep up with the movement of the strong ones but had only drawn themselves out into fine transparent bands, so that back of all was the blue, very clear, but softened."

"I've been reading 'Blithedale,' which I finished last night. Tell me about it. I don't think it is up to Hawthorne's level. What do you think? It seems to me that social and economical subjects are not tenuous enough to slip into the mystery-compartment of Hawthorne's sub-consciousness, and to come out delicately individualized though still typical. This 'Blithedale' is too obviously a type. If it were not, the interest would increase instead of falling off at the middle. I mean to do more reading Hawthorne this summer. Likewise, I will try to get hold of that life of Maurice."

Here is a bit of advice that shows her unusual portion of a humorous common-sense: —

"Don't make yourself think. If you feel that you ought to spur yourself into some thought, choose that of the upper strata. There is plenty of that of which you have not even taken the dip, and you 'll find that it will have its own economic and industrial value. Let the metamorphic rock alone, except to be strengthened by knowing that it is under everything. And of all things don't bore through into the molten interior."

And here, from the same letter, is a perplexed page or two about her own life.

"Now about me, and it will be much me.

I've been much perplexed. What is the proportion of one's duty to one's self and to other people? How know the dividing-line between a selfish egotism, and a cowardly shrinking from assuming the responsibility that one's two talents lay upon one? And how know what one's two talents are? 'The bearings of which observation lies in the application of it.' Here am I, a girl of average mind, nourished for four years on the conventional mental pabulum, with rather more than the average deceptive ability of rhetorical veneering, and of just enough power of self-analysis to perplex myself. More and more each day I realize that I do need a tremendous amount of intellectual ballast to keep me steady. Moreover, I'm not at all sure that I have the energy and concentration and steadfastness to keep up a solitary work. The question, of much preamble, is therefore this: ought I to prepare myself to teach — literature, I suppose? Could I do with writing for an avocation what I could not do with it for a vocation?"

As was suggested by her friend whose words are given above, Clara's early bent had been towards science. The quality of her mind, indeed, was distinctively scientific in accuracy and analytical power. But her nature pressed too near to actual life to find its final home in the remote sphere of science: and she had turned, as this letter shows, less by the deliberate change of intention than by instinct, to a more immediately vital form of thought. The expression of the life of the soul through literature had now become, and remained to the end, the dominant interest of her intellectual life. Desirous of pursuing graduate studies in her specialty, she went to Oxford, England, for the winter of 1884-85. It was during her year at Oxford that the definite conception of a high and arduous scholarship first came to her. In the outward majesty, austere yet lovely, of that "fair city with its crown of towers" she found remoteness from the feverish life of the present, and a revelation of the sacred past that at once soothed and uplifted her spirit: in the mighty Bodleian library, she recognized perhaps for the first time, the value of the pure idea. She plunged into study, specializing on the Elizabethan period. To her amazement, she found standards of work which her abundant cleverness could not satisfy without strenuous effort. Such effort she gave, with spirited and steady devotion. Her work was soon recognized as remarkable for both thoroughness and insight; but it brought her a better reward than outward recognition. She left Oxford with an inward peace not again to be shaken, and with an ideal of scholarship such as few women attain. Seldom, if ever, after this was she content when a generalization was brilliant without asking if it were sound; and it was no longer possible for her to confuse with definite thought the exaltation of emotional suggestion.

The makings of a pedant were not in Clara French. But any danger that her new passion for research and study should lead her away from the needs of average humanity was counteracted by her next experience. After a summer on the heights in Switzerland, she returned to America. No greater change can be imagined than that from the sweetness and light of Oxford to an American Normal School in the country: yet it was as teacher in such a school that she was to spend her next year and a half. Now were manifested the freshness, breadth, and sweetness of her learning. She passed with entire ardor from the subtleties of old English and Elizabethan literature to devising new methods of teaching geography. The years at New Paltz were far from the least happy of her life. The school was new and full of spirit, the surrounding country, at the foot of Lake Mohonk and in full sight of the Catskills, singularly lovely. Although intensely humble and self-distrustful, Clara French grew to know something of the consciousness of power. She inherited the instinct of a teacher, and her work was a delight. Her keen intellect and personal force made themselves felt through the entire school. The second year's teaching brought her much pleasant companionship with other college women employed in the school. The bright busy-ness and energy of the life are well reflected in her letters.

January 15, 1887.

Friday afternoon was the most wonderful time we have had since the snow came. I wish I could make you see it as we saw it. After school we walked up to the top of the hill. The trees were covered and hung with ice, and the clouds were rising from the western hills. When we first looked, the clouds were so low that only one piece of woods was visible on the mountain-side, and that was a soft deep blue, with the cloud-trails still in the tops of the higher trees. Then the clouds rolled farther back, and from behind them fell an almost unearthly pale golden light on the hills, deepening afterward in places to a rose color, while the eastern clouds held their thick, dense blue.

To-day has made an epoch. I've read Amiel, in the translation, I'm sorry to say, but that was at hand, and I had to have something. I sat down after breakfast, and I read till after people came home from church; then I hardly laid the book down during the afternoon. The record of his youth and early manhood, with their subtleties and involutions, and the perpetual failure of coincidence between design and desire, carried me along in sympathy. With increased age, the life becomes more and more pathetic, even tragic in a non-dramatic way, but I feel a little irritation in finding him at fifty substantially where he was at twenty-five; I don't mean in external achievement only, but in his philosophy of life. I shall finish the book to-morrow, and then look forward to the time when I shall re-read it with intervals for thought.

April 17.

I suppose the notes are scholarly, but notes — unless they refer to things historical — have become a weariness to my flesh. The everlasting comment and criticism and inference and explanation I beg to be spared until my present mood is passed. I want to receive in silence what I can of the thought and experience of a great soul, without having some impertinent middleman with all the encyclopædias at his hand, and a kind intent to my edification, step in and remark, "Not so fast, my young reader : x is a sand-hill in the desert of Sahara, and y lived in the farthest Aleutian isle, in the year of grace 1139." If we can't create, leave us at least the privilege of interpreting to ourselves the creations of others. And by way of fitting climax to this tirade, give me "Waring" in a nutshell. Perhaps your diagnosis of my frame of mind towards criticism is the right one. But I'm not sure that I don't find in your ignoring of the individual and deification of all truth a sort of inverted intellectual pantheism.

We've had our two days' vacation, and begun our last stretch of the year. My work is highly amusing, its range being from penmanship to universal history. I have only four classes, and one of them is composed of one man, aged twenty-five. It is English literature. He's the most encouraging material I've had. I gave him some reading to do for one lesson, and he came in with the remark that he had opened the book — one of Carlyle's — at another place, and become so interested that he read his time out and did not turn to my reference. One can do something with a youth who is actually interested in a book.

You should be with us now. The roads are good, and we take long walks again. Yesterday we left home early in the morning, drove to Highland by way of Clintondale, encamped at noon under a big tree and ate our luncheon, and then proceeded to Poughkeepsie. And never in my life did I see so many different kinds of little beasts and birds, with tails and wings, frisking and hopping and flying about, on fences, over stone-walls, by clear brooks, and through the lazy air. And M. showed me all the pretty colors on the hillsides, and in the meadows, and laughed at my attempts to tell what they were made of. And we discussed the condition and possibilities of the farming class, and the relative utility of literature and medicine, and had a delicious, long, lazy morning.

January 30.

The sunset last night was one of the things that one can't describe, that one would not venture even to attempt to describe; but I shall see it always as we saw the whole west from the hilltop. It was the most wonderful sunset that I 've seen here. It was one of the kind that begin a new epoch for one, revealing all one's "sins, negligences and ignorances" in their real ugliness, but giving one a glimpse of the perfection that is not of earth, or of time, and a constraining impulse towards purer living."

In spite of her pleasure in the life at New Paltz, Clara French could not long be satisfied there. Her intellectual hunger, once awakened, was steady and strong, and her desire for further study led her to Cornell University, where she spent her twenty-fifth year in the study of English. Her work during the year, and the impression produced by her scholarship and character, are described for us in a letter from her honored and beloved teacher, Professor Corson: —

THE CORNELL UNIVERSITY.
Department of English Literature.
ITHACA, N. Y., 21 January, 1892.

MY DEAR MISS SCUDDER : —

You ask me to write you a few lines in regard to Miss French's residence at the Cornell University.

Miss French was a resident graduate during the academic year, 1887–88, and received her Master's Degree at the annual Commencement, June 21, 1888.

During my connection with the University up to that time, a period of seventeen years, I had not had a student in my department who did more thorough work, or whose *growth* in certain directions was so rapid.

In addition to her special studies as a graduate student, she took all the regular studies of the department, and was *facile princeps* in all. She read with me extensively in Anglo-Saxon, her reading including the whole of the A.-S. epic of Beowulf, a work of which she was specially fond.

Just before she came to the University, the Mrs. A. S. Barnes Shakespeare Prize had been established, for the best essay on some subject connected with the plays of Shakespeare. This prize was first awarded to Miss French, for her essay here presented on the Play of King John.

Her thesis for the Master's Degree on "Chaucer and Langland as Reflectors of their Age," was the result of a thorough and independent study of her subject.

In a conversation I had with her, on the eve of her leaving the University, I expressed my great satisfaction with what she had done, during the year, and my assurance that she had a most successful career before her as a literary teacher. She asked me what advice I thought she more especially needed, in regard to her future improvement and efficiency in her line of work. I recommended that she should develop and train her voice for an effective vocal interpretation of literature, as I thought such interpretation would do more for her students than any interpretation that could be given through lectures, though the latter had their use. She had an agreeable voice, but it had not received that development and cultivation demanded for the most effective interpretation of the masterpieces of poetic and dramatic literature.

The last letter I ever received from her, she wrote especially to inquire about the methods she should pursue in the vocal culture I had recommended to her, and whether I could assist her in the matter, through correspondence. But a short time after this, I was shocked with the news of her death.

Notwithstanding her splendid record as a

student, the most noteworthy fact connected with her residence at the University was the influence she exerted not only upon the women students with whom she was brought into immediate relationship, but also upon the occupants generally of the Sage College. Many expressed to me their sense of the inspiration they had derived from the high ideals which she was known to cherish, and which she worked conscientiously and enthusiastically to realize.

Her amiability and her genuineness of character endeared her to all with whom she came in contact, and exerted a wholesome influence upon all.

The world lost much by her untimely death. Believe me, my dear Miss Scudder,

Very truly yours,
Hiram Corson.

Miss Vida D. Scudder,
  Boston, Mass.

Clara's scholastic work, centring in her two essays, was, as this letter will show, honest, delicately finished, and sympathetic. Yet such work was in her mind incidental merely to the real gain which this year brought her — the deeper insight into the spiritual revelation of literature, and into the power of art as the free expression of personality. A friend writes an account of the impression she produced in the University : —

"Coming back a few days late to college that year, I was greeted on all sides with word of the new student who was come among us for graduate work. Her scholarly breeding and fine intellectual poise had so soon made her a prominent figure in our college world. We found our own work invested with new dignity and meaning as she went about among us intent on the same studies. Yet we dimly felt that study was to her something finer, better, nobler, than to us, and it was with a sudden sense of awakening that we longed to gain admittance to that rare world in which she seemed to live. She was always willing to help us. Sure of ready sympathy, we brought our essays and translations into her busy days to be criticised with the conscientious thoroughness which marked all she did. She made us all feel a keener liking for study, and to some she was the beginning of that real delight in books and knowledge which will last while life here lasts. Though she never sought to influence by precept or example, I doubt if in all that houseful of life there was another so pervading a personality as hers. We learned to look through her eyes and to adopt her standards, not because she imposed them on us, but because they seemed so supremely right. And in our play as in our work she was the life-centre. Her fun was irresistible, and I have never known so keen and bright a sense of humor, always captivating and never ill-natured. A young woman who was a sophomore that year writes me: —

"'She seemed to stand to me for the best which the term *college woman* may imply, self-controlled and strong and wise; not ignorant of the world and its every-day affairs because of her love for higher things, nor impatient with it, nor discouraged by it, but serene in her belief that the end will be right, and eager to do all in her individual power to bring that right about.'

"To many who knew her but little, she is still

an inspiration and incentive, and to those who knew her best, she is what no words can say.'"

It was a great delight to Clara French when in the early spring of 1888 she received the appointment of Instructor in English Literature at Wellesley College. The position offered her for the first time in her life opportunity for the exercise of the highest powers within her; it was one to which her development for the past eight years seemed consciously or unconsciously to have tended.

She came to Wellesley in September, 1888, grave, silent, her whole nature kindled with ardent and steady devotion. "I can imagine no life," she said, with serious eyes, " more satisfying than that which I am to live at Wellesley."

Within a month, she was withdrawn into the Unseen. The latent power of her nature was to be put forth in no earthly work.

"Look thou not down, but up!
To uses of a cup,
The festal board, lamp's flash, and trumpet's peal,
The new wine's foaming flow,
The Master's lips aglow!
Thou, heaven's consummate cup, what needst thou with earth's wheel?"

In her short life, the evolution of character was swift, clear, and complete. Her nature moved from passion to peace : and the peace she attained was peace, not of stagnation, but of poise. Perhaps she expressed her deepest discovery when she wrote : " It is not in exaltation, but in equilibrium, that strength lies." The over-analytical subtlety that in the old days too often wasted her life-force in twisted thinkings, was replaced by the broader vision that saw life steadily and saw it whole ; she had grown to feel below all surface complexity and confusion the fundamental simplicity of truth. She had developed a singular definiteness of nature ; her powers no longer clashed, but were held in delicate adjustment, ready for instant use. Her sincerity was absolute ; it went deeper than word or thought — it was sincerity of attitude. Perhaps her most striking trait in later years was her absolute self-control ; a control no longer the expression of surface stoicism, but of a firm and quiet soul. So great was this control that it produced in her manner and atmosphere a strange stillness, and in the presence of this stillness restlessness and pain died away. Her nature was serene, with the serenity not of instinct but of conquest, and from her silent strength and cheer there flowed an uplifting power.

Life had grown more to her than speech, and expression became increasingly a matter of the deed, not of the word. Less and less did she brood over the insoluble problems, or waste her vitality in the contemplation of abstractions. To the actual needs of those around her she turned her vision. Some extracts from the letters of her last year will show how nobly practical her introspective and analytical nature had become.

"I find that to shut myself away from the possibilities and opportunities of daily effort and to indulge in an exhaustive outpouring of the profitless side of one's self seems both unnecessary and selfish. I don't speak of such things as we can profitably touch, but of that vast realm of attractive speculation which brings us nothing and leaves us nowhere. I have followed its *ignes fatui* at times through devious ways. I think I shall do so no more.

"The soul has its times of tranquillity, dear,

when the deep places of life are untroubled. And it is not in exaltation but in equilibrium that strength lies."

"I value abstractions, I am roused by problems, but I cannot see that abstraction or problem has any worth, that life has any mystery — what do you mean by life, any way? — except as it involves for good or ill human destiny, and human destiny is the destiny of individuals of the human race. A soul, a life, is to me greater than a formula. The *vital* truths of existence, I think, are comparatively few, and do not depend upon constant, complicated, intellectual processes. As much beyond the fundamental truths as we can get, by all means, but these first; and these with most of us, I fancy, are hardly realized even when reduced to syllogism. You spell truth with a capital, and make of it an independent existence to be sought for and absorbed; but unless truth is God, what can it do for man? It is only a personality that can touch a personality. We are not yet perfect spirits; we are desperately complex beings hampered by the God-given trinity of the world, the flesh, and the devil. To help the world we must take it as we find it, and we find men and women with trivial perplexities and interests ready and longing for the life which is of God, but not to be led to it nor kept in it by an abstruse formula."

"I shall probably continue to think that homely 'available' virtue is better for the world and greater in the sight of the angels above than inefficient exaltation. The homely nature, doing what it sees to do, rises by the doing to greater heights of vision, and at the end does not go down empty-handed. It is a case of doing the will and knowing the doctrine. Such a nature grows constantly strong in spiritual perception and vigor, and begins on this planet to run in the grooves of its eternal development, that is, of productive energy. Of course I prefer the rarer, less tangible qualities in combination with this efficient correlative, but, either alone, I rank the other higher.

"I think we have analyzed too much. Of course you will say just here, 'Professor Corson's influence': granted, but I think it reaches truth. I am undergoing a reaction from that spinning of cobwebs from my own spiritual or intellectual insides which I have indulged in. We have no time for it; we get absolutely nowhere, and meanwhile the realities of our present life press upon us. I think that no soul ever gained a permanent leverage by sitting down and saying, 'Now first I must construct my theory of the universe; afterwards I will use it.' The universe is in the hands of its good Lord, and He does not hold us responsible for its general course. He gives us little things to do, very little things, and in doing them we come to understand somewhat of the sweep of the life of humanity and humanity's God, and to trust Him for what we cannot understand. No laborious labyrinthine pursuit will enable us directly to find ourselves. We must first find others, then we wake and see that the discovery of our important selves was not the thing that was to be sought first. Somewhat modified, perhaps, I am coming to take the position of that familiar bit from Landor: 'I meddle not at present with infinity and eternity; when I can understand them I will talk about them.' Now I know that this seems a low view of life to you. . . . Is it so low? I look back to the Life that was lived eighteen centuries ago by the shores of Galilee, and I find in it, in its deeds and teachings, the perfect warrant for such a view. He did not tell us, 'Thou shalt spend the vital energies of thy threescore years on earth in striving to understand the Lord thy God with all thy intellect.' His commands for this life were simple, very simple; for the next, He Himself will surely care."

These quotations will appear the more unusual when we remember that Clara French, at the time when she wrote them, was pressing forward into an order of intellectual life and work which too often tends to alienate the nature from general sympathy, and to carry it towards isolation.

Her nearer personal interests had become in these last years very definite. The lofty and generally-diffused enthusiasms of her youth had concentrated themselves on three especial lines of energy.

Clara French was a college woman first and foremost. Hers was emphatically the trained nature — trained to such distinctness of self-knowledge, such sense for proportion and nice adjustment of powers as are making of our college women to-day one of the most practical classes in the community. It was inevitable that a large share of her personal interest should be centred in the women's colleges of the country, and in the work of their alumnæ. While feeling keenly the defects and weakness of these colleges and the tentative character of their work, she yet believed with entire loyalty in their ideals, and was ready to place her life-force at their disposal.

Her interest in educational work for women was part of a deeper devotion. It rested on her enthusiasm for disinterested scholarship; a scholarship with no utilitarian end, marked by the distinction of thought which results from clearness, sobriety, and reverence of intellectual vision. The lack of such dynamic scholarship Matthew Arnold signaled as the great defect in our American civilization; scholarship of this order, almost unknown among women, it is perhaps not too much to say that Clara French was on the high-road to attain.

Yet, as her letters clearly indicate, she could never have been contented with an exclusively intellectual life. Life in the concrete had always the strongest claim upon her. It followed that her deepest interest was given to the modern movement towards sociological reform. The movement was less extended five years ago than it is now, and Clara French's life never chanced to bring her within its full sweep; yet her thoughts were tending towards it, and her swift and keen intuition had penetrated to the very heart of the modern method of help. She writes: —

"I'm coming to think that to reach people who are — in some senses — below you, you must touch them first on their own plane, show that you are interested in the things, trivial though they often are, that interest them; and then you can by degrees raise them to your own plane. This mounting a stage, stretching down a hand to some one on the ground, and expecting that person to keep pace with you as you run along, is not practical; it is too much of a strain on the other person's muscles."

The movement which has since crystallized in the establishment of college settlements for women among the poor of large cities was in its infancy in 1888. Clara French's mind was one of the first in which the idea took shape, and with most entire sympathy and steadiest faith did she enter into the earliest efforts of the movement to find realization. The plan for a settlement, indeed, aroused all her most serious enthusiasm. It was a plan for the work of college women: it afforded scope for patient, keen, and broad investigation in that science of sociology which more and more tends to engross the intellect of the day, and it promised to offer a life of as practical and direct consecration to humblest service as even she could desire. Before the plan was realized, she was withdrawn from visible share in its out-working; yet the impulse of her quiet faith and thoughtful hope will not soon pass away.

To reduce a life to a formula is an impossibility; to try to penetrate its essential quality is perhaps not only impossible but wrong. Clara French's own personal experience was direct and simple, yet she gave the impression of one who had touched life at many points, and not only touched but entered. This impression was due to a salient peculiarity of her nature, her strong power of identifying her life with other lives. Sympathetic experience was to her, both in intensity and in depth, what personal experience is to most people. Always ardent in friendship, her nature before the end became almost absolutely selfless. The trouble or the joy of one near to her did not only produce on her a reflex effect; it was her very own, affecting the inmost fibres of her being. Thus she had lived many lives in one, and possessed a breadth and wisdom rare in far maturer years. Fullness of life, intense yet controlled, was the salient fact of her nature. She was one of those people who always make on others a distinct impression, yet whom it is impossible to classify. In spite of her student-life she was not exclusively, perhaps not primarily, an intellectual woman. Nor was she preëminently emotional nor practical, though her nature on both sides was strongly developed. She would have disclaimed for herself with most honest earnestness any striking spirituality of nature. Faith, strong though silent, lay at the heart of her noble womanhood; but of the mystic she had nothing. With a steadfast humility she said, in the last months of her life: "I am one of the plain, every-day people of this world, with only occasional glimpses of another. I trust indeed that it may be so

>"'That earth may gain by one man the more,
> And the gain of earth shall be heaven's gain too.'"

By no peculiarity of nature did Clara French impress herself on others. Yet her effect in many lives can never be effaced. It was due not to her gifts but to herself; to the very vigor and movement of her personality, to the intensity of the life that shone through her. Her nature was once described as a clear and steady flame; and it had indeed not only the radiance, but also the purity and the aspiration of fire.

Her grave is in the shadow of great oak-trees at Syracuse, New York. The cross that rises above it bears the words, —

"Rejoice and be glad with her, all ye that love her: rejoice for joy with her, all ye that mourn for her."

VIDA D. SCUDDER.

THE
DRAMATIC ACTION AND MOTIVE OF KING JOHN

AN ESSAY FOR THE MRS. A. S. BARNES
SHAKESPEARE PRIZE

D. C. — 68.

NOTE. The references to the Troublesome Raigne of King John are to the page of the reprint of the old play in Hazlitt's Shakspere's Library, Part II. Volume I.; those to Shakespeare's King John are to the act, scene, and line of the Globe Shakespeare.

THE
DRAMATIC ACTION AND MOTIVE OF KING JOHN

IN turning from the study of character and psychological motive in Shakespeare to that of dramatic action there is at first a haziness of understanding of the new point of view. Our familiarity with the plays blinds us to new aspects of them; we see in them only what we have been used to see. Accordingly we may perhaps in the case of one play make clearer the meaning of the dramatic action and the outworking of the dramatic motive by a running comparison with a play comprehending the same events and characters but of inferior dramatic workmanship. The Troublesome Raigne of John, King of England, a play by an unknown author, first printed in 1591, may thus serve as a foil to Shakespeare's King

John. A careful reading of this earlier play fails to disclose in it a legitimate dramatic motive. Its purpose, so far as any one controlling purpose can be discovered, is to exhibit in proportions and colors as hateful as possible, the corruption and tyranny of the Romish Church. It has several distinct currents of events, but they converge to no dramatic end. It has a long succession of episodes, but there runs through them no combining purpose. This spirit of anti-Romanism, violent as it is, — and of its violence we shall have proof further on, — is not artistically embodied in concrete form; it is rather enforced by a series of sledge-hammer blows, their only unity being that they are struck from the same shoulder, and hit the same spot. Shakespeare's King John has, however, an unmistakable dramatic purpose, we might almost say a series of concentric purposes, the immediate concrete end being involved in the broader and deeper motive. The right of John to the throne, the inmost political motive, is secondary to the exhibition of his cowardice, selfishness and greed, and the train of calamities in which these passions involve other persons and the whole nation ; and both these ends are, in turn, made to show forth that keen patriotism with which the England of Elizabeth tingled in every nerve. For these motives, severally, the old play gives us a succession of political artifices and deceits ; a confused assemblage of persons bound by no organic tie ; and a circumscribed insularity of nationalism.

We may consider briefly the differences in the dramatic presentation of the two plays and the significance of the most important of these differences. It is to be noticed at the outset that Shakespeare made no essential changes in the plot of the early play. If there is no play in which Shakespeare departs further from authentic history, there is also none in which he follows more closely the outline of events laid down in his original. But by an omission here, an addition there ; by throwing one scene into the background through narration, by bringing a narrated action forward upon the stage; now by severing a relation between two characters and now by making that relation closer,—by such changes of construction, each in itself slight, Shakespeare has wrought into indissoluble unity a mass of diverse elements.

It may be said in general that the most obvious of Shakespeare's changes in scene and speech are for condensation, compression and compactness, tending to unity. Thus we see that in the first scene the King and Faulconbridge are at once brought into closer relation by John's direct address to Philip and his brother Robert, " What men are you ? " without the mediation of Essex, who in the earlier play is made to question the brothers. The writer of the earlier play makes Lady Faulconbridge enter with her two sons, and the discussion of Philip's paternity is begun in her presence before the entire court, though the brutality of Philip's threats is reserved until he is alone with his mother. In Shakespeare the dispute between the two brothers and the knighting of Philip precede Philip's first characteristic soliloquy, after which Lady Faulconbridge and James Gurney enter. Gurney is immediately dismissed, having uttered only one speech of four words : —

"Good leave, good Philip."[1]

which, as a side-light upon Philip's previous character and position, are worth a volume of commentary, and Philip and his mother are left alone. The greater delicacy of Shakespeare's arrangement is immediately obvious, as is also the stage economy, by which the stage is cleared of a part of its crowd of actors, and a slight variety is imparted to the view.

In the Shakespearean version Philip is also given the opportunity further to reveal himself in soliloquy.

The entire episode between Philip and Austria is greatly shortened by Shakespeare. In the earlier play the interest is distracted from the main theme of the drama by the frequently renewed dispute between these hot-blooded nobles, — if we can fairly call Austria hot-blooded, who is brave in taunts but cowardly in blows. They have a sharp preliminary skirmish of words; Philip chases Austria and makes him leave the lion's skin; the nuptial arrangements are interrupted by the challenge from Philip to Austria and the conferring of

[1] Act I. Sc. i. 231.

the Dukedom of Normandy upon Philip. All this confuses the action during the meeting of the kings, the parley with the citizens, and the forming of the marriage-contract. It is the intrusion of a second action at a time when the main one is at a highly critical juncture. Notice, on the other hand, that in Shakespeare these skirmishes between Philip and Austria are carried on to later scenes and always appear as entirely subordinate issues. Shakespeare binds the several actions together and strengthens the chief one by making Philip take an important part in the main action, proposing the league of the kings, whereas in the old play Philip is so engrossed with his own quarrel that he places himself quite out of the main current of events. Shakespeare also strengthens the dramatic complication by bringing Constance and Arthur prominently forward in these scenes, while in the old play they are but two of the crowd of figures on the stage. In the old play, too, there is here introduced a touch of gallantry between Philip and Blanche, with the inference that Elinor had promised Blanche to Philip in marriage. Shakespeare's

Philip, however, never appears as even a possible lover. To present him in this guise would be to destroy the consistent simplicity of the part he has to play in the national action of the drama. In the Troublesome Raigne, Philip kills Austria on the stage and tramples upon his body in the very ferocity of revenge, uttering at the same time a soliloquy relating to his personal affairs alone. In Shakespeare Philip enters with Austria's head, but his words are of the fortunes of the day as affecting the English cause. Shakespeare never destroys the continuity of dramatic progress by introducing at any time irrelevant issues.

Immediately after the killing of Austria the old playwright brings Elinor on the stage as the prisoner of Lewis, and there follows a taunting of Elinor by Constance in a vein of exulting spitefulness which shows how different was his conception of Constance from Shakespeare's: —

> "Constance doth live to tame thy insolence,
> And on thy head will now avenged be
> For all the mischiefes hatched in thy brain.

My time is now to triumph in thy fall,
And thou shalt know that Constance will triumph."[1]

To a modern ear the spitefulness of the taunt is much emphasized by the position of the accent of the last word, but no difference of orthoepic standard could make the invective mild. After this passage in the old play John rescues Elinor, and Arthur is taken prisoner. Shakespeare's changes here subserve several dramatic purposes. He avoids the choppiness of this too frequent change of scene, preserves the dignity of the Queen Mother, and forbears interfering with the rush of the dramatic current, by introducing Arthur as already taken and by narrating in two lines Elinor's capture and her rescue, the rescue, let it be noted, being accomplished not by John, but by Philip.

The scene of the plundering of the Priory, which in the old play is remarkable for its very liberal humor, has no counterpart in the Shakespearean play. Here again the contents of several pages are expressed in a few lines: —

"How I have sped among the clergymen,
The sums I have collected shall express."[2]

[1] Act I. Sc. i. 257-8.   [2] Act IV. Sc. ii. 141.

This is Shakespeare's equivalent for a scene that brings forward several characters who appear nowhere else, and disfigures the play by its low humor and the virulence of its religious partisanship.

A comparison of the scene between Hubert and Arthur in the two plays would include the very interesting study of the contrast between Shakespeare and the earlier dramatist in character drawing, a study in which would be noticed especially the changing of John from an unscrupulous coward and liar to the victim of the more subtle weakness, irresolution, and fear of Shakespeare's king; the refining of Constance from a clamorous virago to a wronged and sorrowing mother; and the raising of Philip from a blustering bully to a strong, true-hearted Englishman. But it is with the dramatic action that we have now to do, and we can consider only such points as bear directly upon this subject. An indirect bearing all the changes referred to have, of course, in bringing the drama to an equipoise of moderation and in preserving our sympathy for each of its characters; but other changes pertain more closely to the dramatic construction. In the scene between Hubert and Arthur, then, and indeed in the person of Arthur wherever he appears, one thing is to be especially noticed, his youth as compared with the Arthur of the Troublesome Raigne. The Arthur of the old play appeals personally to the citizens of Angiers for the recognition of his rights as sovereign, and argues with Hubert with the subtlety and coolness of a practiced dialectician. The reader cannot help feeling that if the boy be blinded, his powers of disputation will stand him very well in the place of one sense. There is really no pathos in this earlier scene. But Shakespeare, simply by reducing the boy's age so that he can have no political ambitions for himself, makes him the unconscious centre of one phase of the political action of the play, and the occasion of all that part of the drama in which Constance stands as the defender of his helplessness. The bearing of this slight change on the entire movement of the play is of very great importance.

The second coronation of John, which in the

old play is performed on the stage in dumb show, Shakespeare narrates; and finally a significant change occurs in the poisoning and death of the king. In the earlier play the plot for the poisoning is laid on the stage by the monk and abbot; John is poisoned at a banquet at which Philip is present, though the latter is warned in time against the fatal drink; the monk dies from his draught, and Philip kills the abbot. All this sanguinary excess Shakespeare does away with, partly of course because the stage representation of it would destroy the effect of the death-scene of the king, and also in order to eliminate the violent religious element, and to avoid an extreme degradation of the king's person. These are the chief differences in dramatic presentation between the Troublesome Raigne and Shakespeare's King John. The element of soliloquy in Shakespeare's play, so useful in revealing Faulconbridge to us, is throughout, as in the first scene, his own addition. Now these changes, as has been said, are made not only at the dictate of a higher refinement than that of the unknown earlier author, not only to express the genius of a greater poet, but, first and last, to fulfill the conditions of distinctively dramatic art. In the earlier play the groups of which Arthur, Philip and John are the centres, are more or less separate and independent; the currents of events in which they are actors move along side by side, but join rarely save in mere external contact. In Shakespeare the destinies of the principal characters are so interwoven that the play would fall in pieces if one of them were taken out. Shakespeare's original is a mosaic, his own play an organic structure. So too in the matter of stage effect we have glanced at Shakespeare's superiority, his economy of material, his use of the principle of contrast, his skill in compact construction, his restraint in subordinating minor effects to dramatic climaxes.[1]

Helped, perhaps, by this comparison, we may briefly consider the dramatic purpose and movement of Shakespeare's play alone. The

---

[1] The suggestive paper on "Shakespeare as an Adapter" by Mr. Edward Rose, in *Macmillan* for November, 1878, came to my knowledge too late to be of service in writing this essay.

opening scene sets before us the ground of the war with France, John's usurpation, on which, for the first part of the play, depends the dramatic movement.

"The borrowed majesty of England here."[1]

says Chatillon, and Elinor, left alone with John, says to him: —

"Your strong possession much more than your right,
Or else it must go wrong with you and me:
So much my conscience whispers in your ear,
Which none but heaven and you and I shall hear."[2]

The action of the play proceeds, "to rebuke," as Lewis says to Arthur,

"the usurpation
Of thy unnatural uncle, English John."[3]

The supporters of Arthur's claim have an absolute belief in his right to the throne: —

"We'll lay before this town our royal bones,
Wade to the market-place in Frenchmen's blood,
But we will make it subject to this boy."[4]

This is the French King's resolve, and when John approaches he meets him with: —

[1] Act I. Sc. i. 4.   [2] Act I. Sc. i. 40.
[3] Act II. Sc. i. 9.   [4] Act II. Sc. i. 41.

> "But thou from loving England art so far,
> That thou hast under-wrought his lawful king,
> Cut off the sequence of posterity.
> . . . .
> That Geffrey was thy elder brother born,
> And this his son; England was Geffrey's right,
> And this is Geffrey's." [1]

It is worthy of remark that John nowhere denies his usurpation, but seeks to outface his accusers with bold words:—

> "From whom hast thou this great commission, France,
> To draw my answer from thy articles?" [2]
> "Doth not the crown of England prove the King?" [3]

But he is very glad to escape the necessity of fighting for his crown, and he accedes with alacrity to the marriage of Blanche to Lewis and the dowry of Anjou, Touraine, Maine and Poictiers. It is the clear-sighted Faulconbridge who recognizes the falseness and injustice of this compact in his soliloquy, —

> "Mad world! mad kings! mad composition!" [4]

John now defies Pandulph and is excommunicated. At this point the two lines of dramatic action represented here by Pandulph

---

[1] Act II. Sc. i. 94 *seq.*
[2] Act II. Sc. i. 110.
[3] Act II. Sc. i. 273.
[4] Act II. Sc. i. 56.

and Constance join; Rome and France, with more or less insincerity and juggling on the part of Rome, remain for a time now allied against England. It is Constance who in her loneliness first makes common cause with Pandulph:—

"O, lawful let it be
That I have room with Rome to curse awhile!
Good father Cardinal, cry thou amen
To my keen curses; for without my wrong,
There is no tongue hath power to curse him right.
　Pandulph. There's law and warrant, lady, for my
　　curse.
　Const. And for mine too: when law can do no right,
Let it be lawful that law bar no wrong:
Law cannot give my child his kingdom here,
For he that holds his kingdom holds the law;
Therefore, since law itself is perfect wrong,
How can the law forbid my tongue to curse?"[1]

Pandulph bids Philip of France let go John's hand,

"And raise the power of France upon his head,
　Unless he do submit himself to Rome."[2]

France is perplexed and seeks to find a middle course; but urged by the Dauphin on the

[1] Act III. Sc. i. 105.　　[2] Act III. Sc. i. 193.

one hand and Constance on the other, with the curse of Rome impending over him he yields : —

"England, I will fall from thee."[1]

and the effect of his decision on the two parties is voiced by Constance and Elinor : —

"*Const.*   O fair return of banish'd majesty!
Elinor.   O foul revolt of French inconstancy!"[2]

John has now arrayed against him France and Rome, France directly and Rome indirectly because of his usurpation. Between John and the undisturbed possession of the throne stands the person of the rightful heir. All will go well, it seems to John, if Arthur can be finally put out of the way, and as soon as the fortunes of war make the boy his prisoner, he takes steps for his disposal. The short scene in which the king darkly intimates to Hubert his wishes concerning his nephew is in certain ways the most wonderful in the play. The significance of the suspension of the verse while the king is striving to utter his wish, his monosyllabic breathings as he gains courage to voice it definitely, and his final gratuitous

[1] Act II. Sc. ii. 320.   [2] Act III. Sc. ii. 321.

lightness, — these features give to the scene a sombre, evil power which marks it as a rare height in dramatic expression.

Arthur is sent to England in Hubert's keeping, and the dramatic prevision of his fate comes to us from the mouth of the wily Pandulph in a dialogue with Lewis the Dauphin : —

> "And therefore mark.
> John hath seized Arthur ; and it cannot be
> That, whiles warm life plays in that infant's veins,
> The misplaced John should entertain an hour,
> One minute, nay, one quiet breath of rest.
> . . . .
> That John must stand, Arthur needs must fall;
> So be it, for it cannot be but so." [1]

And further on : —

> "O, sir, when he shall hear of your approach,
> If that young Arthur be not gone already,
> Ev'n at that news he dies: and then the hearts
> Of all his people shall revolt from him,
> And kiss the lips of unacquainted change,
> And pick strong matter of revolt and wrath
> Out of the bloody fingers' ends of John.
> Methinks, I see this hurly all on foot." [2]

In this way, by what we may call dramatic

---

[1] Act III. Sc. iv. 136 *seq.*   [2] Act III. Sc. iv. 169.

prophecy, we are prepared for the main course of the events that fill the rest of the play.

The shadow of the dark cloud that wraps in the close of the drama soon begins to fall. After John's second coronation the lords request Arthur's enfranchisement, which the king ostensibly grants, only to announce, soon afterwards, the child's supposed death. The lords utter their suspicions of foul play, John's misfortunes are increased by the death of his mother and the landing of the French. Hubert is sent to assure the lords that Arthur lives, and the prince leaps from the walls to give the lie to Hubert's assurance.

To the original dramatic motive, John's usurpation, is now added another, the death of Arthur, and the combined force of the two hastens the play to its sad end. The last act of the drama is taken up with the irresistible rush of the current of destiny. There is no point at which the sweep of events could be stayed, there is no spot at which light breaks through the gloom. The act opens with John's final abasement in yielding himself to Pandulph. Town after town receives the French

King, John's nobles desert him and ally themselves with his enemy, Philip loses half his force, and the king is poisoned and dies. But before his death the revolted nobles have returned to him, and the faithful Philip is beside him at the last.

Such, then, is the outworking of the dramatic motive of King John in its main line of movement. With this main plot is wrought an underplot consisting of the series of actions of which Pandulph is the centre. The deceit and treachery of John to establish himself on the throne find an echo in the deceit and treachery of Pandulph to gain supremacy over England and France. The chief political motive is thus emphasized by a parallel religious motive, the latter, it must be borne in mind, being always subordinate. It is interesting also to notice the way in which the characters of the play are bound together for dramatic effectiveness; their relations to each other and to the main current of the play; the interweaving of actions; the organic connection of episodes. These are briefly presented below in the form of an analysis of the plot of King

John based upon the canons of dramatic criticism laid down by Mr. Richard G. Moulton in his "Shakespeare as a Dramatic Artist." Certain of the technical terms suggested by Mr. Moulton have been replaced by a more familiar phraseology, in order that the analysis may be self-explanatory. The single term "passion drama" may need a slight explanation. It is Mr. Moulton's substitute for the conventional term tragedy. Says the author: "The true distinction between the two kinds of plays is one of movement, not tone. . . . Thus in these two kinds of dramas the impression which to the spectator overpowers all other impressions, and gives individuality to the particular play, is this sense of intellectual or of emotional unity in the movement, — is, in other words, action-movement of passion-movement. The two may be united, — but one or the other will be predominant and will give to the play its unity of impression. The distinction, then, which the terms comedy and tragedy fail to mark would be accurately brought out by substituting for them the terms action-drama and passion-drama."

KING JOHN.

A PASSION-DRAMA.

Scheme of Actions.

Main Nemesis Action ; Usurpation of John and its consequences.

Underplot : an Intrigue Action ; Machinations of Pandulph to subdue England and France to Rome, parallel with machinations of John to secure firmly the English crown.

Double Tragedy : Main Nemesis Action ; John undone by what seemed his safety.

Tragic Action : Constance and Arthur ; Suffering and death of the innocent.

Character Sub-action : Faulconbridge, extending throughout the play.

Sub-Action at Rise of Dramatic Complication ; Lewis and Blanche. (Act II. Scene i.)

Sub-Action at Crisis of Dramatic Complication : Hubert and Arthur. (Act IV. Scene i.)

Sub-Action during Catastrophe : Salisbury, Pembroke and Bigot, — their desertion and return. (Act IV. Scene ii. 4.)

Enveloping Action : Wars and Treaties with France and Rome.

Oracular Action: Peter of Pomfret's prophecy (Act IV. Scene ii.) enforced by prodigy of five moons. (Act IV. Scene ii.)

Ironic Elements of Action : the king's extreme precaution in commanding the death of Arthur and in allying himself with Rome proves his ruin ; Arthur's death comes from himself, after the revocation of the king's command to Hubert; the treachery of the revolted nobles is checked and they are turned again to loyalty by the treachery of one of their French allies, Melun.

External Circumstance : Disclosure of Philip's paternity. (Act I. Scene i.)

Economy.

Two chief parties, French and English, linked by common personages, Arthur and Pandulph.

Interweaving : by episodes of Philip and Austria, Blanche and Lewis (Act II. Scene i.), English lords, Lewis and Melun, (Act IV. Scene ii. 4.)

Envelopment in common enveloping action.

Contrast as an enforcing bond: Arthur the rightful king, whose life is sought, dies by accident; John the usurping king, who endeavors to confirm his own position by Arthur's death, dies poisoned by a subject.

Character contrast between John, the throned king, base, cowardly, and treacherous, and Philip, the son of Cœur-de-Lion, the embodiment of the national spirit.

Movement.

Passion-Movement with convergent motion.

Turning-Points.

Centre of Plot: Capture of Arthur (Act III. Scene ii.); John's apparent success the cause of his final ruin.

Catastrophe: Culminating Nemesis, from Arthur's supposed death, and the announcement of Elinor's death and of the preparations of the French (Act IV. Scene ii.), continuing through Act V. to the death of the king.

THE NATIONAL SPIRIT AS EMBODIED IN FAULCONBRIDGE.

THE search for "types" in Shakespeare is often misleading. It frequently involves the disregard of many facts of dramatic presentation and the distortion of others. Worse than this, it fosters the tendency to stamp a character with a formula and to ignore its individuality. Nevertheless there are certain characters whose individuality is strongly marked and whom at the same time it is difficult to escape from feeling that Shakespeare intended to stand as representatives or ideals of a temper and spirit that comprehends more than themselves. Perhaps it is reading a somewhat overwrought history into the drama to say that the historical plays contain more of these representatives than the other plays. It is, however, a commonplace of criticism that there runs through the series of English historical plays, a high and enthusiastic national spirit, and this spirit we find occasionally caught up and embodied in a concrete form in some one character. Just this is done by the character of Faulconbridge in King John. The time of the play, as Professor Dowden has said, is that of "the utmost ebb in the national life of England." Cruelty, treachery, and weakness darken the scene. Subjects forget their allegiance, the king trifles away his honor. But one true-hearted Englishman remains near the throne, and to him turns all the loyalty and in him shines forth all the patriotism of England.

See how English he is in what we have grown to regard as distinctively national traits, even in the faults to which some of them tend. He is always direct, outspoken, blunt. He wastes no hour in words when deeds are needed, and is at any time somewhat irritated to find himself the subject of open praise. When Hubert, with a mild, involuntary expression of respect calls him "brave soldier," he interposes, —

"Come, come, sans compliment, what news abroad?"[1]

Moral ostentation he cannot away with, and anything approaching religious seriousness he turns aside with a smile and a shrug. To Elinor he says, —

> "Grandam, I will pray,
> If ever I remember to be holy,
> For your fair safety; so, I kiss your hand."

Even with his mother in the first scene he shows the same roughness and bluntness, though he spares her the brutal threats by which Philip in the earlier play extorts a confession from Lady Faulconbridge.

> "Madam, I was not old Sir Robert's son,"

he begins at once, but not, as has been noticed, until Gurney is sent away. Yet what we feel in his roughness is never a rude lawlessness, but rather an unsubdued strength. His courage and contempt of cowardice are constantly made manifest. He rouses the cowardly and sinking king with a shock of vigorous contempt, —

> "But if you be afeared to hear the worst,
> Then let the worst unheard fall on your head."[2]

[1] Act V. Sc. vi. 16.   [2] Act IV. Sc. ii. 135.

His British courage first finds vent in arms, and he is, while the times demand soldiership, thoroughly a soldier. He loves fair play, and stands resolutely between Hubert and Salisbury on the discovery of Arthur's death, though he afterwards treats Hubert to a torrent of indignation on his own part. When Salisbury draws his sword, Philip stays him : —

"Your sword is bright, sir; put it up again.
 Salisbury. Not till I sheathe it in a murderer's skin.
  . . . .
Thou art a murderer.
 Hubert.   Do not prove me so.
Yet I am none : whose tongue so'er speaks false,
Not truly speaks ; who speaks not truly, lies.
 Pembroke. Cut him to pieces.
 Bastard.   Keep the peace, I say."[1]

But after the lords go out, Philip utters this magnificent hyperbole of indignation : —

"*Bastard.* Here's a good world : Knew you of this
 fair work?
Beyond the infinite and boundless reach
Of mercy, if thou didst this deed of death,
Art thou damn'd, Hubert.
 Hubert.   Do but hear me, sir.

[1] Act IV. Sc. iii. 79 *seq.*

Bastard.   Ha: I'll tell thee what;
Thou 'rt damn'd as black — nay, nothing is so black;
Thou art more deep damn'd than Prince Lucifer:
There is not yet so ugly a fiend of hell
As thou shalt be, if thou didst kill this child.
  Hubert. Upon my soul —
  Bastard.   If thou didst but consent
To this most cruel act, do but despair;
And if thou want'st a cord, the smallest thread
That ever spider twisted from her womb
Will serve to strangle thee; a rush will be a beam
To hang thee on; or would'st thou drown thyself,
Put but a little water in a spoon,
And it shall be as all the ocean,
Enough to stifle such a villain up." [1]

Philip is at all times the man of action, prompt, decided, energetic. In the midst of his dispute with Austria the king gives an order for action, and Philip drops at once his personal quarrel, ceases for the time to be the son of Plantagenet, the victim of Austria, and becomes the son of Plantagenet, King of England.

> "Up higher to the plain; where we'll set forth
>   In best appointment all our regiments," [2]

---

[1] Act IV. Sc. iii. 116 *seq.*   [2] Act II. Sc. i. 105.

says John, and Philip is forthwith England's soldier : —

"Speed, then, to take advantage of the field."

So when the king at last in conscious weakness hands over his authority to Philip with the words, —

"Have you the ordering of this present time,"[1]

Philip accepts the trust unhesitatingly, and having failed to arouse and encourage the king to act for himself, bids him, now that the command is in stronger hands, —

"Away then, with good courage."

Philip has, too, a thoroughly English sense of humor. It does not consist, like the humor of the French, in intellectual hair-breadth escapes, but is of a merrier sort, delighting in the general aspect of an amusing situation, though having at times withal a half melancholy undertone. In almost his first speech he gives a humorous turn to his pious wish, —

"Heaven guard my mother's honor and my land."[2]

His quick retort to Queen Elinor shows his ready wit.

---

[1] Act V. Sc i. 77.   [2] Act I. Sc. i. 70.

"*Bastard.* Madam, I'll follow you unto the death.
Elinor. Nay, I would have you go before me thither.
Bastard. Our country manners give our betters way."[1]

The bombastic citizen of Angiers affords him exquisite amusement.

"Here's a large mouth, indeed,
That spits forth death and mountains, rocks and seas,
Talks as familiarly of roaring lions
As maids of thirteen do of puppy-dogs:
What cannoneer begot this lusty blood?
He speaks plain cannon fire, and smoke and bounce;
He gives the bastinado with his tongue;
Our ears are cudgell'd; not a word of his
But buffets better than a fist of France."[2]

And Lewis's perfunctory love-speech sets him off into a conceit which it is a pity that Lewis himself cannot hear:—

"Drawn in the flattering table of her eye!
Hang'd in the frowning wrinkle of her brow!
And quarter'd in her heart! he doth espy
Himself love's traitor; this is pity now,
That, hang'd and drawn and quartered, there should be
In such a love so vile a lout as he."[3]

These lesser English traits, directness, courage, promptness, and single-heartedness in action,

[1] Act I. Sc. i. 154.   [2] Act II. Sc. i. 455 *seq.*
[3] Act II. Sc. i. 504.

contempt of affection, and a wholesome humor are supplemented in Philip by the English national pride. Nor is there in this anything of the British braggadocio to which the intense nationalism of some of Shakespeare's contemporary dramatists came dangerously near. It is the honest, hearty, fervent glow of that love for country which England has never felt in greater warmth than she felt it in the days of Elizabeth. This is the undertone in all his words, the ground and end of all his actions. His first words in the play prepare us for the part that we see him sustain throughout.

"What men are you?"

asks the king of the brothers, and Philip replies, —

"Your faithful subject, I,"[1]

and a faithful subject he is always, even when his allegiance must be to the crown alone, not to its wearer. Elinor sees at once in him "some tokens" of her great son, and "the very spirit of Plantagenet;" he denies himself a Faulconbridge "as faithfully as he denies the

[1] Act I. Sc. i. 50.

devil;" and when he has wrung from his mother his father's name, he takes high pride in the thought that he is not the son of old Sir Robert, but of the great Cœur-de-lion:—

> "Ay, my mother,
> With all my heart I thank thee for my father!"[1]

In deriving his descent thus from the king who made great the name of England in foreign lands, Philip appears at the outset as a fit person to embody the national spirit and to gather to himself the loyalty of his countrymen when perforce it falls away from the one to whom it should cling. This descent is also emphasized in the quarrel with Austria, when Philip stands as the avenger of his father's death. His position as a directing force in the play is first made manifest at the meeting of the kings before Angiers. Philip of France and King John made long, ineffective speeches; there is much of excursions, heralds, trumpets; the kings pompously assert their claims, but still the citizens refuse either of them entrance:—

[1] Act I. Sc. i. 269.

"A greater power than we denies all this;
And till it be undoubted, we do lock
Our former scruple in our strong-barr'd gates;
King'd of our fears, until our fears, resolved,
Be by some certain king purged and deposed." [1]

This passive defiance is too much for Faulconbridge. Silent before, save for his slight passages with Austria and his one short speech of ready energy, —

"Speed then, to take advantage of the field,"

he now bursts forth before either of the kings can invent another indecisive speech: —

"By heaven, these scroyles of Angiers flout you kings,
And stand securely on their battlements,
As in a theatre, whence they gape and point
At your industrious scenes and acts of death.
Your royal presences be ruled by me." [2]

He then presents his plan of union between the kings for the reduction of the town and for the subsequent settling of the rival claims by battle, ending with, —

"How like you this wild counsel, mighty states?
Smacks it not something of the policy?" [3]

[1] Act II. Sc. i. 369 *seq.* [2] Act II. Sc. i. 373 *seq.*
[3] Act II. Sc. i. 395.

and John, always willing to shirk a responsibility, replies at once, —

> "Now, by the sky that hangs above our heads,
> I like it well."[1]

The Bastard's plans are frustrated by the "mad composition" which the kings soon make, but by his readiness for action and the soundness of his counsel he has been placed before us as the exponent of saner loyalty, courage, and judgment than those of England's king.

His part in the scene in which John is excommunicated is slight, but a greater confidence is given to the English cause when, after the king has said, —

> "France, thou shalt rue this hour within this hour,"[2]

Philip repeats his words with a preliminary play, —

> "Old Time the clock-setter, that bald sexton Time,
> Is it as he will? well then, France shall rue."[3]

Before he goes to England on the king's commission to collect money for the war,

---

[1] Act II. Sc. i. 397.   [2] Act III. Sc. i. 323.
[3] Act III. Sc. i. 324.

Philip appears, in the short scene already referred to, as the rescuer of Elinor. During his absence from John, the king performs his most dastardly act, and gives Hubert the command for Arthur's death. A selfish and cowardly remorse for this deed has just seized the king, when a messenger announces to him the approach of the French power and the death of his mother. The weak king is for a moment left alone, without the imperious strength of his mother or the faithful support of his kinsman, the Bastard, and he reels in bewilderment:—

> "Thou hast made me giddy
> With these ill tidings."[1]

At this point Philip returns, strong, controlled, and hopeful, and the spirit of English steadfastness is breathed over the scene. He gives the king a chance to deny his part in the supposed murder of Arthur, but the king only sends him, his fears of John's baseness confirmed, to appease the angry noblemen:—

[1] Act IV. Sc. ii. 131.

> "I have a way to win their loves again,
> Bring them before me.
>
> . . . .
>
> Be Mercury, set feathers to thy heels,
> And fly like thought from them to me again."[1]

Philip's brief reply, with this confirmation of the king's guilt before him, is

> "The spirit of the time shall teach me speed,"

and he goes on, to do his utmost towards setting right what is wrong. When he meets the noblemen he guards his words from even the appearance of disloyalty, until the sight of Arthur's dead body forces from him the judgment:—

> "It is a damned and a bloody work;
> The graceless action of a heavy hand,"

adding in the same breath, however,—

> "If that it be the work of any hand."[2]

Finally, the lords having left, he utters his only confused or disheartened sentence, shows that he well understands the actual condition of England, and before he finishes, takes upon himself consciously the burdens of the time.

[1] Act IV. Sc. ii. 168.   [2] Act IV. Sc. iii. 57.

> "Go, bear him in thine arms.
> I am amazed, methinks, and lose my way
> Among the thorns and dangers of this world.
> How easy dost thou take all England up!
> From forth this morsel of dead royalty,
> The life, the right and truth of all this realm
> Is fled to heaven; and England now is left
> To tug and scramble and to part by the teeth
> The unowed interest of proud-swelling state.
> Now for the bare-pick'd bone of majesty
> Doth dogged war bristle his angry crest,
> And snarleth in the gentle eyes of peace:
> Now powers from home and discontents at home
> Meet in one line; and vast confusion waits,
> As doth a raven on a sick-fall'n beast,
> The imminent decay of wrested pomp.
> Now happy he whose cloak and centre can
> Hold out this tempest. Bear away that child
> And follow me with speed: I'll to the King;
> A thousand businesses are brief in hand,
> And heaven itself doth frown upon the land." [1]

This is our only glimpse of an abatement of hopefulness on Philip's part, and even here he commands himself at once and we know him to be prepared for whatever may follow. What does follow is of all things the most saddening

[1] Act IV. Sc. iii. 139 *seq.*

to a loyal Englishman — his king gives further proofs of baseness and cowardice, and reveals the "inglorious league" made with the Pope's legate. A foreign power dictates to the king on English soil and the king speaks of his humiliation as a "happy peace" — this marks the disappearance of the king as in any sense a national representative, and Faulconbridge from this point on becomes the sole embodiment of the national spirit. But his loyalty to the king as king remains unimpaired, he is still the "faithful subject" of the first scene of the play. The vigorous lines beginning

"But wherefore do you droop? Why look you sad?"[1]

are his last effort to raise the king to the height of a kingly mind and conduct. To this stirring speech, the king replies only with a declaration of the making of the peace, and Philip urges a last motive for action: —

"Perchance the cardinal cannot make your peace:
Or if he do, let it at least be said
They saw we had a purpose of defence."[2]

The king thereupon commits to Philip "the

[1] Act V. Sc. i. 44.   [2] Act V. Sc. ii. 74.

ordering of this present time" and Philip becomes the recognized leader of the English, himself, however, always paying reverence to that kingly ideal which bears sway over him. In the scene with Pandulph and Lewis, Philip's patriotism is on fire. The Roman legate has brought England to a depth of submission to which France will not descend, and the Dauphin, on English ground, refuses to lay down his arms against England's twice-crowned king.

"He flatly says he'll not lay down his arms," [1] reports Pandulph of Lewis, and Philip flames forth his white-hot burst of indignant defiance:

"By all the blood that ever fury breathed,
  The youth says well. Now hear our English King;
  For thus his royalty doth speak in me.
  He is prepared and reason too he should:
  This apish and unmannerly approach,
  This harness'd mask and unadvised revel,
  This unhair'd sauciness and boyish troops,
  The King doth smile at; and is well prepared
  To whip this dwarfish war, these pigmy arms,
  From out the circle of his territories." [2]

[1] Act V. Sc. ii. 126.   [2] Act V. Sc. ii. 127.

More in the same vein follows and Philip closes his message with this: —

> "For at hand,
> Not trusting to this halting legate here,
> Whom he hath used rather for sport than need,
> Is warlike John; and in his forehead sits
> A bare-ribb'd death, whose office is this day
> To feast upon whole thousands of the French."[1]

Notice that throughout these speeches Philip, though intrusted with the fortunes of the time, assumes for himself nothing: he is the king's messenger, — "I am sent to speak," "from the king I come," he says; and he brings forward the king as the emblem of a power and temper which now in the eyes of foes and friends reside in him alone, — "Now hear our English King," "at hand is warlike John." Here too he is still the "faithful subject."

Finally near Swinstead Abbey Philip meets Hubert and learns from him of the king's poisoning. Half of his own power has been meanwhile "devoured by the unexpected flood" in Lincoln Washes, the day begins to look desperate, and his one eager wish is to be conducted

[1] Act V. Sc. ii. 174.

to the king; here he must relate his disasters and offer the support of his presence and counsel. He reaches the king "scalded with the violent motion" of his haste, and begins to tell his story, but while he is speaking John dies.

Philip first gives utterance to his loyalty to the king: —

> "Art thou gone so? I do but stay behind
> To do the office for thee of revenge,
> And then my soul shall wait on thee to heaven,
> As it on earth hath been thy servant still."[1]

Then he comes back to the thought of his country, of which the king has been to him the visible symbol, and calls upon the stars to

> "return with me again
> To push destruction and perpetual shame
> Out of the weak door of our fainting land."[2]

But the cardinal has at last reduced the Dauphin to subjection and the preparations for war are given over. King John's burial is arranged for, and Philip tenders his allegiance to the new king: —

> "And happily may your sweet self put on
> The lineal state and glory of the land!

[1] Act V. Sc. vii. 70.   [2] Act V. Sc. vii. 77.

> To whom, with all submission, on my knee
> I do bequeath my faithful services
> And true subjection everlastingly."[1]

With this his part in the play ends. He has revealed himself throughout as the representative of the distinctively English traits of character and habits of mind. He has held on high, when in other hands it has been extinguished, the torch of a glowing patriotism. He has drawn to himself the feelings of national loyalty and pride which, on his own part, he always directs towards the sacred ideal of the kingly office embodied for him in the unworthy John. Shakespeare has elsewhere, in the person of Henry V., drawn for us the man whom he would have us receive as the typical English King, "the hero and central figure of the historical plays;" but the atmosphere of royalty about him removes him somewhat from the sphere of other Englishmen. In Philip the Bastard, however, the national spirit is presented still more forcibly in one below the throne. Son though he is to Cœur-de-lion, royalty has no allurements for

---

[1] Act V. Sc. vii. 101.

him; as he enters, the "faithful subject" of King John, so, having borne on his own shoulders the burdens of John's reign, he leaves, bequeathing to John's son his "faithful services and true subjection everlastingly." It is fitting that from his strong English heart should come the superb nationalism of the close of the play:—

"This England never did, nor never shall,
  Lie at the proud foot of a conqueror,
  But when it first did help to wound itself.
  Now these her princes are come home again,
  Come the three corners of the world in arms,
  And we shall shock them. Nought shall make us rue,
  If England to itself do rest but true."[1]

[1] Act V. Sc. vii. 112.

A COMPARISON OF THE TROUBLESOME RAIGNE OF JOHN, KING OF ENGLAND, AND SHAKESPEARE'S KING JOHN,

AS EXHIBITING THE SHAKESPEARIAN NON-PARTISAN SPIRIT.

In the first part of this essay a brief comparison was made between the dramatic workmanship of Shakespeare and that of the author of the Troublesome Raigne of King John. A comparison of the spirit of the two writers is of still more interest, as explaining in great measure their differences in artistic excellence. The contrast between them is exhibited most markedly in their respective attitudes toward Romanism, and it is, therefore, to their treatment of the religious element in the plays that we look for evidence of their breadth and justice of spirit.

This contrast is first expressed in their general plan of dramatic construction. Though the old play can hardly be said in strictness to have an informing purpose, yet as has been pointed out, its pervading spirit is that of anti-Romanism. It seems to have been written largely as a dramatic exhibition of the English hatred of Rome, and it is certainly a forcible expression of the passion of religious bigotry. We may notice a few of the dramatic milestones, especially in their bearing upon the religious spirit of the play. The opening scenes of the old play are of a somewhat heterogeneous character, war, inconstancy, revenge, and gallantry succeeding each to each; but the predominant tone is at the outset political, in a "swashing and a martial" fashion. With the entrance of the "Cardynall from Rome,"[1] however, begins the true life of the play. Here we have King John and the Cardinal speaking "plain cannon fire, and smoke, and bounce," each giving the other "the bastinado with his tongue" in unstinting measure. We are made at once to feel that, whatever the relative im-

[1] Page 254.

portance of the other issues of the play, the contest between king and cardinal is of supreme moment. The French king ranges himself unhesitatingly on the side of Rome, and all powers obnoxious to England are forthwith barred off in a common compartment for convenience of odium.

"Brother of Fraunce, what say you to the Cardinall?"

asks John, and France answers, —

"I say, I am sorrie for your majestie, requesting you to submit your selfe to the Church of Rome."

John proceeds, —

"And what say you to our league, if I do not submit?"

to which the king's prompt reply is, —

"What should I say? I must obey the Pope."[1]

And after John and his train have left the scene, France assures Pandulph of his devotion to Rome with the words, —

"Pandulph, thy selfe shalt see,
How Fraunce will fight for Rome and Romish rytes."[2]

The contrast of the old writer with Shake-

[1] Page 256.   [2] Page 256.

speare in these scenes has already been implied. Shakespeare makes the primary national interest of the drama unmistakable from the beginning. Faulconbridge, the central character, is identified with the patriotic current; the meeting before Angiers presents in brief the problems of the play; and the entrance of Pandulph we feel to be an intrusion, of great and ominous significance indeed, but an intrusion, and not the first appearance of one of the two great forces of the play.

The hesitation of the French king to break his oath and ally himself with Rome is also in sharp contrast to his ready and unquestioning adherence in the Troublesome Raigne.

"I am perplexed and know not what to say,"[1]

he says, and after a clear statement of the injustice of the proposed compromise and alliance he adds, —

"O holy sir,
My reverend father, let it not be so!
Out of your grace, devise, ordain, impose
Some gentle order; and then we shall be blest
To do your pleasure and continue friends."[2]

[1] Act III. Sc. i. 221.   [2] Act III. Sc. i. 248.

It is only after much persuasion that he yields and falls from England.

The single portion of the drama wherein the two playwrights differ most obviously and markedly is, of course, the priory scene with its related circumstances. In Shakespeare's play the king's command to Faulconbridge is this : —

> "Cousin, away for England! haste before;
> And ere our coming, see thou shake the bags
> Of hoarding abbots. Set at liberty
> Imprison'd angels ; the fat ribs of peace
> Must by the hungry now be fed upon.
> Use our commission in his utmost force." [1]

And Philip makes a brief reply, mocking, and, as often, misrepresenting himself : —

> "Bell, book and candle shall not drive me back,
> When gold and silver becks me to come on." [2]

Hear now the king of the earlier play. At the beginning of hostilities he declares : —

> "Ile ceaze the lasie Abbey lubbers lands
> Into my hands to pay my men of warre.
> The Pope and Popelings shall not grease themselves
> With gold and groates, that are the soldiers due."

[1] Act III. Sc. iii. 6.   [2] Act III. Sc. iii. 12.

And he gives his commission to Philip in these words: —

> "But leauing this we will to England now,
> And take some order with our Popelings there,
> That swell with pride and fat of lay mens lands
> Philip, I make thee chiefe in this affaire,
> Ransack the Abbeys, Cloysters, Priories,
> Conuert their coyne unto my soldiers use:
> And whatsoere he be within my land,
> That goes to Rome for justice and for law.
> While he may haue his right within the Realme,
> Let him be judged a traitor to the State
> And suffer as an enemie to England." [1]

Philip's reply here is: —

> "Now warres are done, I long to be at home,
> To dive into the Monks and Abbots bags
> To make some sport among the smooth skin nunnes
> And keepe some reuell with the fanzen Friers." [2]

In the dialogue between Pandulph and Lewis, Shakespeare again reminds us that

> "The bastard Faulconbridge
> Is now in England, ransacking the church,
> Offending charity." [3]

[1] Page 259.
[2] Page 260.   [3] Act III. Sc. iv. 171.

But of the results of his commission we have only the two lines quoted above.

> "How I have sped among the clergymen,
> The sums I have collected shall express."[1]

The Troublesome Raigne, however, gives a long and disgusting scene as a specimen of the process of collecting these sums. Philip enters, "leading a Frier, charging him show where the Abbots golde lay."

> *Philip.* Come on you fat Franciscan, dallie no longer, but show me where the Abbots treasure lyes, or die.
> *Frier.* *Benedicamus Domini*, was euer such an injurie?
> Sweete S. Withold of thy lenitie, defend us from extremitie,
> And heare us for S. Charitie, oppressed with austeritie
> *In nomine Domini*, make I my homilie,
> Gentle gentilitie grieue not the cleargie.
> *Philip.* Gray-gownd good face, conjure ye, nere trust me for a groate
> If this waste girdle hang thee not that girdeth in thy coate.
> Now bald and barefoote Bungie birds, when up the gallowes climing,
> Say Philip he had words inough, to put you down with ryming."[2]

[1] Act IV. Sc. ii. 141.   [2] Page 262.

The friar begs for mercy, and Philip grants it when the promise of conduct to the prior's chest is made him. The friar warrants the chest to hold "a thousand pound in silver and in gold," but when the coffer is opened it is found to contain not silver and gold, but "faire Alice the Nun." Philip comments on the discovery in very execrable verse, and agrees to accept, as ransom for fair Alice, the hoard of an ancient Nun. Again, however, he finds not treasure, but Friar Lawrence, a fact which forces from him more bad verse and worse sentiments, and he leaves, after giving the order to bind the offenders and "haste them to execution."

In the following scene a side touch is given in the remark of Peter the prophet, here represented as a "dissembling knaue" of the fortune-telling type: "I must dispatch some business with a Frier, and then Ile read your fortunes."[1]

And further on, when Philip makes report to the king, John in delight at Philip's intimation, —

[1] Page 266.

"I doubt not when your Highness sees my prize,
  You may proportion all their former pride," —

says, —

" Why so, now sorts it Philip as it should:
  This small intrusion into Abbey trunkes,
  Will make the Popelings excommunicate,
  Curse, ban, and breath out damned orisons,
  As thick as hailestones fore the spring's approach:
  But yet as harmless and without effect,
  As is the echo of a cannons crack
  Discharged against the battlements of heaven."[1]

But Shakespeare introduces Peter of Pomfret, in a short passage in which Philip is made to declare of him to the king, —

"he sung, in rude harsh-sounding rhymes
  That, ere the next Ascension day at noon,
  Your highness should deliver up your crown."[2]

Peter is sent to prison, with the king's command for his hanging at noon of the day mentioned, and the apparition of the five moons is announced later by Hubert, neither prophecy nor prodigy being made of ecclesiastical import. In Shakespeare's original, however, the apparition of the moons is presented on the

---

[1] Page 273.   [2] Act IV. Sc. ii. 150.

stage, and Peter is summoned from the presence door, where he has been left by Philip, to interpret the omen for the king. He fulfills the command in this manner : —

> "The skies wherein these moones have residence,
> Presenteth Rome the great Metropolis,
> Where sits the Pope in all his holy pompe.
> Foure of the Moones present four provinces,
> To wit, Spaine, Denmarke, Germaine, and France,
> That bear the yoke of proud commanding Rome,
> And stand in feare to tempt the Prelates curse.
> The smallest moone that whirles aboute the rest,
> Impatient of the place he holds with them,
> Doth figure foorth this Island albion,
> Who gins to scorne the See and State of Rome,
> And seekes to shun the edicts of the Pope." [1]

And further on, "by some other knowledge that he has," "by his prescience," Peter foretells the dispossession of the king on Ascension Day.

After Arthur's death and Philip's announcement of the election of Lewis by the nobles, John, in the old play, finds himself "a mad man," his "hart mazd," his "senses all foredone" and Philip, before going to plead with

[1] Page 276.

the nobles, reflects upon the cause of his mishaps : —

> "I goe, my lord : see how he is distraught,
> This is the cursed Priest of Italy
> Hath heapt these mischiefes on this hapless land." [1]

John left alone, revolves the course of action he will adopt with the cardinal when he appears : —

> "The Pope of Rome, 't is he that is the cause,
> He curseth thee, he sets thy subjects free
> From due obedience to their Soveraigne :
> He animates the Nobles in their warres,
> He gives away the Crowne to Philip's sonne,
> And pardons all that seeks to murther him :
> And thus blind zeale is still predominant.
> Then John there is no way to keepe thy Crowne,
> But finely to dissemble with the Pope:
>
> . . . .
>
> Thy sinnes are farre too great to be the man
> T' abolish Pope and Poperie from thy Realme." [2]

And he dissembles, alternately crouching to the legate and defying him under his breath.

> "For Priests and Women must be flattered." [3]

But when the news of the approach of the

---

[1] Page 291. [2] Page 291. [3] Page 292.

French fleet is brought to him, he becomes "reconciled unto the church" and meekly accepts the "sound aduise" of Pandulph.

Shakespeare, on the other hand, avoids emphasizing the religious element by opening the fifth act just as the king submits to the cardinal: —

> "Thus have I yielded up into your hand
> The circle of my glory." [1]

And throughout the remainder of the play Shakespeare's John finds only a "happy peace" in this degradation. But the king in the old play takes occasion to revile himself for his concession: —

"The Deuil take the Pope, the Peeres and Fraunce:
Shame be my share for yeelding to the Priest." [2]

Next after the priory-scene the death-scene of the king exhibits most sharply the contrast between the spirit of the two authors as it is manifested in their treatment of the religious element of the play. In the old play the motive of this scene is still anti-Romanism. Much is made of the preparations of the monks

---

[1] Act V Sc. i. 1. [2] Page 305.

for poisoning the king. When John reaches Swinstead and the abbot has assured him of such welcome as the Abbey can afford, Philip, mindful of the king's sickness, says, —

> "The King thou seest is weake and very fainte,
> What victuals hast thou to refresh his Grace?"

The abbot answers, —

> "Good store, my Lord, of that you neede not feare,
> For Lincolnshire, and these our Abbey grounds
> Were neuer fatter, nor in better plight."

Whereupon John recovers sufficiently from his weakness and faintness to address Philip in this manner : —

> "Philip, thou neuer needst to doubt of cates,
> Nor King nor Lord is seated halfe so well,
> As are the Abbies throughout all the land,
> If any plot of ground do passe another,
> The Friers fasten on it straight:
> But let us in to taste of their repast,
> It goes against my heart to feed with them
> Or be beholden to such Abbey groomes."[1]

All the characters but one monk now leave, and the monk soliloquizes : —

> "Is this the king that neuer lov'd a Frier?

[1] Page 309.

Is this the man that doth contemne the Pope?
Is this the man that robd the holy Church,
And yet will flye into a Friory?
Is this the King that aymes at Abbeys Lands?
Is this the man whom all the world abhorres,
And yet will flie into a Friorie?
Accurst be Swinstead Abbey, Abbot, Friers,
Monks, Nuns, and Clarks, and all that dwell therein,
If wicked John escape aliue away.
Now if that thou wilt look to merit heauen,
And be canonized for a holy Saint:
To please the world with a deseruing worke,
Be thou the man to set thy countrey free,
And murder him that seeks to murder thee."[1]

The abbot enters, and the monk breaks to him his purpose.

"What if I say to strangle him in his sleepe?"

The abbot, fearing that the monk is mad and means to murder him, begs for his life, or, if that cannot be spared, for time to say his prayers. He is speedily reassured by the monk, to whom he then listens.

"Wilt thou not hurt me, holy Monke? say on.
Monk. You know, my Lord, the king is in our house.
Abbot. True.

[1] Pages 309, 310.

Monk. You know likewise the King abhors a Frier.
Abbot. True.
Monk. And he that loves not a Frier is our enemy.
Abbot. Thou saist true.
Monk. Then the King is our enemy.
Abbot. True.
Monk. Why then should we not kill our enemy, and the King being our enemy, why then should we not kill the king.
Abbot. O blessed Monke! I see God moues thy minde to free this land from tyrants slauery. But who dares venter for to do this deede?
Monk. Who dare? why I my Lord dare do the deede, Ile free my Country and the Church from foes,
And merit heauen by killing of a King." [1]

The monk is absolved by the abbot, "for why the deede is meritorious," and he goes about his work. The scene of the poisoning contains much detail, from the entrance of " two Friers laying a cloth " to the king's wretched death. When the king declares that he is poisoned, Philip breaks out in a fury, and fells the abbot:—

"This Abbot hath an interest in this act.
At all adventures take thou that from me.

[1] Pages 311, 312.

> There lye the Abbot, Abbey, Lubber, Diuill.
> March with the Monke unto the gates of hell." [1]

John's last words are a prophecy of evil to Rome: —

> "My tongue doth falter: Philip I tell thee man:
> Since John did yeeld unto the Priest of Rome,
> Nor he nor his haue prospered on the earth:
> Curst are his blessings, and his curse is blisse
> But in the spirit I cry unto my God,
> As did the Kingly Prophet David cry,
> (Whose hands, as mine, with murder were attaint)
> I am not he shall build the Lord a house,
> Or roote these locusts from the face of the earth:
> But if my dying heart deceive me not,
> From out these loynes shall spring a Kingly braunch
> Whose arms shall reach unto the gates of Rome,
> And with his feete treads down the Strumpets pride,
> That sits upon the chaire of Babylon." [2]

Young Henry soon enters, saying, —

> "O let me see my father ere he dye:
> O Uncle, were you here, and suffered him
> To be thus poysoned by a damned Monk?" [3]

And after his father's death his appeal to Philip is, —

---

[1] Page 315. [2] Page 316. [3] Page 317.

> "Sweete Uncle, if thou loue thy Soveraigne,
> Let not a stone of Swinstead Abbey stand,
> But pull the house about the Friers ears,
> For they haue killde my Father and my King."

Thus the close of the play is animated by the same spirit of fierce hatred to Rome that is displayed in all the earlier scenes. Contrast now the utterly different spirit of the close of Shakespeare's play. The poisoning scene is omitted entirely, and in its place we have but these lines, spoken by Hubert to Philip:—

"The King, I fear, is poison'd by a monk,
I left him speechless, and broke out
To acquaint you with this evil, that you might
The better arm you to the sudden time,
Than if you had at leisure known of this.
    Bastard. How did he take it? who did taste to him?
    Hubert. A monk, I tell you: a resolved villain,
Whose bowels suddenly burst out: the King
Yet speaks, and peradventure, may recover."[1]

There is here none of the detail of the plotting of the monks, and later there is no final malediction by the king, no appeal for revenge from the young prince. All partisan tones are

[1] Act V. Sc. vi. 23.

suppressed, and in their place sounds the dignity of a strong patriotism.

We have seen, then, at different stages in the progress of the drama, how entirely opposed is the spirit of one writer to that of the other. At the dramatic crisis of the older play it is the spirit of anti-Romanism that shapes the course of events; in Shakespeare's play the religious element is never more than an undercurrent, a secondary agency in determining the dramatic progress; and when it does enter into the play it is introduced as any other modifying factor, not with the shrill bitterness which always attends it in the earlier drama.

Further, the Troublesome Raigne has several distinct characters representing different aspects of the Romish monster: Shakespeare's play has neither monk, abbot, friar, nor nun; the cardinal legate is here the sole representative of Rome. The contrast between the cardinals of the two plays, moreover, gives additional emphasis to the different attitudes of the writers. The cardinal of the Troublesome Raigne is a galvanized creature, responding at a touch with the perfunctory words of his office. He walks stiffly through the play, uttering his pious formulæ, banning or blessing, as the occasion demands. He is always mindful of the dignity of his red hat. At his first appearance he makes long speeches that sound like the tedious utterances of a legal document. Later, when the French king speaks of Austria, just dead, the cardinal is ready with his familiar form of words: —

> "His soule is safe and free from Purgatorie,
> Our holy Father hath dispensed his sinnes,
> The blessed Saints haue heard our Orisons,
> And all are Mediators for his soule." [1]

He answers the summons of the king, and when the latter has servilely submitted himself to him, he says, —

> "No, John, thy crouching and dissembling thus
> Cannot deceiue the Legate of the Pope." [2]

But upon John's further protestation he professes to see the king's hearty penitence, and comforts him with the assurance that, let him

> "But yet be reconcil'd unto the church,
> And nothing shall be grieuous to thy state." [3]

[1] Page 260.   [2] Page 292.   [3] Page 293.

So again at the refusal of France to make peace with England, he draws himself up to say, —

> "Then in the name of Innocent the Pope,
> I curse the Prince and all that take his part,
> And excommunicate the rebell peeres
> As traytors to the King and to the Pope."[1]

And finally at John's death-scene he comes forward in a professional manner, and, having exhorted the king to forgive the revolted lords, addresses him : —

> "K. John, farewell : in token of thy faith,
> And signe thou dyest the servant of the Lord,
> Lift up thy hand."

Here as always it is the cardinal who speaks, not the man. There is nothing human about him, nothing interesting. He is the wearer of the dress of the Church, the automatic speaker of the Church's words, a lay figure merely, to serve as a target for the hate of other personages in the play. And this hate he does not fail to call forth at their first meeting. John says to him : —

[1] Page 304.

"And what hast thou or the Pope thy maister to doo to demand of me, how I employ mine own? — Tell thy maister so from me, and say, John of England said it, that neuer an Italian Priest of them all, shal either haue tythe, tole, or polling penie out of England: but as I am King, so will I raigne next under God, supreame head both ouer spiritual and temprall: and he that contradicts me in this, Ile make him hoppe headlesse."[1]

And after his excommunication he is hotly defiant: —

"So sir, the more the Fox is curst the better a fares: if God blesse me and my Land, let the Pope and his shauelings curse and spare not."[2]

Shakespeare's cardinal, however, is much more than a portrait of a dignitary of the Church. He is the keen, clear-sighted ecclesiastical politician, used to "look quite through the deeds of men," and to manipulate princes and potentates to the Church's advantage. He understands when to command, as with Philip of France,[3] when to reason and persuade, as with the Dauphin.[4] His life is a life of plot and intrigue. He says to Lewis, —

"How green you are, and fresh in this old world!"[5]

---

[1] Page 255. [2] Page 255. [3] Act III. Sc. i.
[4] Act. III. Sc. iv. [5] Act III. Sc. iv. 145.

And we feel that he himself is "in this old world" most thoroughly seasoned. It is to him in Shakespeare also that the most violent partisan speeches of the play are made, but the figures of Friar Lawrence and Friar Francis interfere to prevent us from regarding Pandulph as Shakespeare's embodiment of Romanism. And even these partisan speeches have nothing of the ring of the corresponding speeches of the old play. After the legate's opening question, the king replies: —

"What earthy name to interrogatories
Can task the free breath of a sacred king?
Thou canst not, cardinal, devise a name
So slight, unworthy and ridiculous,
To charge me to an answer, as the pope.
Tell him this tale; and from the mouth of England
Add thus much more, that no Italian priest
Shall tithe or toll in our dominions;
But as we, under heaven, are supreme head,
So under Him that great supremacy,
Where we do reign, we will alone uphold,
Without the assistance of a mortal hand:
So tell the pope, all reverence set apart
To him and his usurp'd authority." [1]

[1] Act III. Sc. i. 147.

The contrast between this and the earlier "and he that contradicts me in this, Ile make him hoppe headlesse," needs no comment. France now ventures a slight expostulation, to which John returns: —

> "Though you and all the kings of Christendom
> Are led so grossly by this meddling priest,
> Dreading the curse that money may buy out;
> And by the merit of vile gold, dross, dust,
> Purchase corrupted pardon of a man
> Who in that sale sells pardon for himself,
> Though you and all the rest so grossly led
> This juggling witchcraft with revenue cherish
> Yet I alone, alone do me oppose
> Against the pope, and count his friends my foes."[1]

These, together with Hubert's reference to the "resolved villain," are the most vehement outbursts against Romanism that Shakespeare's play contains. And the defiance to the Pope voiced in these speeches and elsewhere is simply defiance to a foreign power, not to an ecclesiastical system as such, — to this the whole current of the play bears witness. No part of Philip's speech in Act IV., Scene ii., —

[1] Act III. Sc. i. 162.

"By all the blood that ever fury breath'd," etc., is directed against Rome, though Pandulph has just failed in his embassy of peace; nor do we anywhere find a subordination of the patriotic interest to the ecclesiastical.

The extortions of the friars, their avariciousness, inactivity, gluttony, and sensuality, and the rapacity and tyranny of the Pope, — these are the features of Romanism beyond which the author of the Troublesome Raigne cannot see. He never loses a chance to thrust at the officers and customs of the Church, and many of his thrusts take the form of the childish spitefulness of calling names, — "lazie Abbey lubbers," "fat Franciscan," "gray-gownd good face," which lowers the dignity of the anti-Romish party and helps to vulgarize the whole play.

In the early play, too, the spirit of anti-Roman partisanship is faintly echoed by an insularity of self-glorification which takes the places of the patriotic nationalism of Shakespeare's play. The traditional feud between Frenchmen and Englishmen flashes out in occasional comparisons that reveal the partisanship of nationality, as the main current of the play reveals the partisanship of religion.

Shakespeare, however, is great enough to see the essential truth underlying local abuses. He has entirely eliminated the partisan spirit from this play, and given it instead as an enveloping motive "a firm manly national sentiment to which all may respond." His artistic restraint grows out of his true catholicity in all things. It is because he is the symmetrical man whom we know that he can be the great artist whom we are beginning to recognize.

www.ingramcontent.com/pod-product-compliance
Lightning Source LLC
Chambersburg PA
CBHW022144160426
43197CB00009B/1417

9783743377325